(America Before Columbus)

A Play for Young People

by

JOSEPH ROBINETTE

I. E. CLARK, Inc.
Schulenburg, TX 78956

Printed in the United States of America

ISBN 0-88680-212-1

A*B*C*

(America Before Columbus)

Cast

Sam (or Sally), the stage manager

Asha, a young girl

Baloe, a young boy

Ensemble Chorus

The **Chorus** is flexible. As few as seven or as many as 30 may be used to enact the numerous characters and episodes in this one-hour presentation of the 20,000-year history of America before Columbus. The **Chorus** may be all male or all female or any combination thereof.

In the text, numbers are arbitrarily assigned to chorus members (Actor 1, Actor 2, etc.) merely as a suggested guide for dividing the dialogue among the Chorus Members. The director may reassign the speeches at his/her discretion. The numbers are not meant to be consistent throughout the play; that is, "Actor 1" in the first scene does not have to be the same performer as "Actor 1" in the next scene.

NOTES ON THE PLAY

Who discovered America? Why, Columbus, of course! But wait . . . weren't there people on the shore to greet him when he arrived? And what about all that evidence that other Europeans had reached America before Columbus?

*A*B*C**, by one of America's best-known authors of scripts for children's theatre, is cleverly written and arranged to entertain child audiences with humor and action while teaching them something about the prehistory of the continent. The performers may be children or adults, or some of each. With very little scenery (a few cubes or boxes), *A*B*C** is ideal for touring.

The author suggests simple basic costumes of modern casual attire—blue jeans, sweat shirts, T-shirts, sneakers. Additions to the basic costume can suggest the various characters and animals (ears and horns to symbolize a buffalo, for example). Other types of costumes may be used, but the author is opposed to dressing all the characters in stereotyped caveman or early Native American costumes. The play is symbolic, not realistic. The author adds:

"There are virtually no ground rules for the director in this 'open theatre' approach to a very unusual subject—the REAL discovery of America."

Joseph Robinette is Director of Children's Theatre at Glassboro, N. J., State College. The author of 38 produced plays, he received the 1976 Chorpenning Cup, awarded annually by the American Theatre Association to an outstanding nationally known writer of children's plays.

*A*B*C** was well tested before publication, with professional productions at the Barter Theatre, Abingdon, Va.; A Company of Players, Jacksonville, Fla.; and the Maryland-National Capital Park & Planning Commission which toured to 75 Baltimore area schools; and with non-professional productions at several high schools and colleges, including the University of Wisconsin-Whitewater and Appleton, Wis., West High School. Here are some comments to use in your publicity releases:

"The play is working extremely well... Resident director Owen Phillips—who joined Barter way back in 1935—came to the play and left raving about it, stating that it is the best children's script he has seen produced at the Barter."—Ken Robbins, Barter Theatre

"*A*B*C appealed to me upon first reading because it not only was a fun script, but because it was a teaching tool as well... [It is] certainly a show which tours easily... I've always contended that the true test of a good children's show is its appeal to a wide range of ages & types & here *A*B*C** fills the** (cont. on p. 40)

A*B*C*

(America Before Columbus)

[Several cubes of various dimensions stretch from Up Right to Down Left. The cubes will be used in many combinations throughout the play to become such diverse locales as the home of the cliff-dwellers, mounds of the Mound Builders, and, at the beginning, as the Bering Strait. Several folding screens are located upstage. When the actors are not part of the action, they will go behind the screens, although the director may wish to simply suggest exits by having actors turn away from the action and stand upstage.

AT RISE: the houselights dim to half as a spot or "special" comes up Down Right. Stepping into the light is SAM (or SALLY) the Stage Manager. He is holding a clipboard and may be wearing a set of headphones. Although a bit nervous, he is in control]

SAM. Good morning (afternoon or evening). Welcome to our play. My name is Sam (Sally). I'm the Stage Manager. Most of you probably don't know what a stage manager does. Well, for one thing he starts the play. He tells the actors when to go on stage. He tells the lighting people which lights to turn on and off. *[He gives hand signals; the spotlight obeys]* If an actor is nervous and wonders what comes next, he goes to the Stage Manager and whispers– *[very loud]* "What comes next!?" Yes, the Stage Manager has lots of duties, but there's one job he doesn't like to do. And that's the one I'm doing right now–talking to you. Oh, don't get me wrong. I like *talking* to you. It's the *reason* I'm talking to you that I don't like. You see, if everything were ready, I wouldn't even be out here right now. I'd be backstage saying to the actors–"Places, please." That means get ready for the show. So, why am I not backstage saying, "Places, please"? I'll tell you. The actors aren't here yet. Oh, they're on their way. But until they arrive, who has to keep things going so you don't get bored? Me, good old Sam, the Stage Manager. Well, let me start by telling you a little about today's play. It's all about the discovery of America. *[Moving into the stage area as the stage lights come up to half]* You'll have to use your imagination quite a bit this morning– *[wryly]* especially if the actors don't get here. *[He goes to the cubes (see Floor Plan, p. 40)]* First of all, these boxes aren't just boxes. They'll be mountains, caves, hiding places and lots of other–

[From the rear and/or sides of the auditorium or from backstage, the ACTORS appear and yell, "We're here!"] Hello! *[Pleasantly, with a touch of sarcasm]* We're so glad you could come.

[The ACTORS rush down the aisles. They are carrying trunks and boxes loaded with props and costume pieces, if desired; however, the boxes and trunks may already be onstage. The ACTORS speak ad lib to the audience:]

ACTORS. Sorry we're late. / We lost our road map. / Got held up by the train. / The boys are such slow-pokes. / It took the girls an hour to get ready. / We'll just be a minute. / Bear with us. / This is so embarrassing. *[Etc., ad lib, as they ascend the stage. One ACTOR crosses to Sam]*

ACTOR. Are you the Stage Manager?

SAM. Yes, my name's Sam. *[All greet him as they hurriedly don costume pieces]* Please hurry now. We're late already.

ACTORS. Okay, okay. / We're almost ready. Etc.

SAM. All set?

ACTORS. Yeah. / We're set. Etc.

SAM. Places, please. Begin the show!

[The house lights go out as the stage lights come up full. SAM exits Down Right. ACTORS 1, 2, 3, 4, and 5 step forward as each very dramatically delivers his/her line (numbers are assigned to the actors for convenience. Each director may re-assign the numbers to fit his/her cast):]

ACTOR 1. Hello, allow me to introduce myself. I am Christopher Columbus.

ACTOR 2. And I am Queen Isabella of Spain.

ACTOR 3. I am the captain of the great ship Pinta.

ACTOR 4. And I'm a no-good sailor on the Santa Maria.

ACTOR 5. I am the first Indian to greet Christopher Columbus when he discovers–

SAM. *[Entering]* Wait a minute–wait a minute–cut– *[To the audience]* "Cut" means stop. *[To the actors]* I'm sorry, but I thought this play was about the discovery of America.

ACTOR 1. It is. *[Dramatically]* I am Christopher Columbus.

ACTOR 2. I'm Queen Isabella.

ACTOR 4. I'm a no-good sailor on the Santa–

SAM. Yes, yes, I know. But the *real* discovery of America–the one we're set up for–began a long time before Christopher Columbus.

ACTOR 3. It did?

ACTOR 1. How long before Christopher Columbus?

SAM. About 20,000 years before.

ACTORS. *[In unison]* Twenty-thou–!

ACTOR 3. We can't do a 20,000-year play in one hour.

SAM. You can't do *everything* that happened, but you can act out a few of the interesting things.

ACTORS. *[Not sure]* I don't know about this. / This isn't what we planned at all. / I don't think we can do it. Etc.

ACTOR 5. Sam, we don't even know about America before Columbus. *[The others agree]*

SAM. Well, the audience probably doesn't either. And that seems to me a pretty good reason for doing it.

ACTOR 2. He may be right.

ACTOR 1. Let's talk about it.

ACTOR 3. Excuse us, please. *[They huddle]*

SAM. *[Wearily]* The job of a Stage Manager is no bowl of M and M's I tell you. *[The ACTORS break the huddle]*

ACTOR 1. Sam, we agree it might be fun to do a play about the real discovery of America, but there's one problem.

SAM. What's that?

ACTOR 1. No play.

SAM. Then we'll improvise. *[To the audience]* "Improvise" means we'll make it up as we go along.

ACTOR 5. But how?

SAM. *[Indicating the clipboard]* I have some notes here that may help.

ACTOR 3. Notes?

SAM. Sure, when I heard you were doing a play about America, I studied up on the subject and made some notes.

ACTOR 4. Great! Where do we start?

SAM. How about–at the beginning?

ACTOR 2. Terrific idea. Why didn't I think of that?

SAM. Okay, all set? Now, according to my notes, there was a time–many years ago when–

ACTOR 4. Shucks.

ACTOR 5. What's wrong?

ACTOR 4. I wanted to be–a no-good sailor on the Santa Maria.

SAM. In the play we're going to improvise, you'll get to act many parts—be many people.

ACTOR 4. Yeah?

SAM. Good people, not-so-good people, even animals.

ACTOR 4. Okay, but I want to be at least one not-so-good person.

SAM. I guarantee it. Now, as I was saying—there was a time, many years ago, when ice and snow covered much of America. And nobody—nothing else—was here.

ACTOR 3. Not even a McDonald's?

ACTOR 2. *[Gouging him]* Shhh!

SAM. Nothing at all. Just snow— *[The ACTORS mime falling snow with their fingers]* And ice— *[The ACTORS are "frozen"]* And chilling winds— *[They make sounds of wind]*

ACTOR 1. Was there anybody anywhere in the world?

SAM. Oh, yes. There were some people in Asia.

ACTOR 5. Asia? Is that close to Philadelphia? *[NOTE: Any city or town may be substituted]*

SAM. Asia is another country. To the northwest, it's next to America. The Asians were the first people to come to this country.

ACTOR 5. How did they get here?

ACTOR 2. In airplanes, silly.

ACTOR 3. Airplanes? Twenty thousand years ago?

ACTOR 2. Yeah. I guess that was a little before airplanes. How about . . . trains?

ACTOR 1. She's hopeless. They came in . . . boats?

SAM. Nope.

ACTOR 3. They swam?

SAM. They walked.

ACTOR 5. From Asia? You can't walk to America from Asia.

SAM. You can't today. But you could then.

ACTOR 5. How?

SAM. By crossing the Bering Strait.

ACTOR 2. What's the Bering Strait?

SAM. Today it's water. But back then it was a little piece of land—actually more like a path of ice—that connected Asia and Alaska.

ACTOR 1. Alaska? You mean the state—Alaska?

SAM. Exactly. Of course it wasn't a state then. There were no states. Or America. It was just—this land.

ACTOR 2. What should we call it then?

ACTOR 4. How about Acirema?

ALL. Acirema?

ACTOR 4. That's America spelled backwards.

ALL. *[Giving him the business]* Aw, go on. / That's ridiculous. Etc.

ACTOR 5. Let's call it North Mexico. *[ALL stare at him]* Well, we are–north–of Mexico. Forget it.

ACTOR 1. How about East Asia.

ACTOR 3. But we're west of Asia.

ACTOR 1. No, we're not. We're–

ACTOR 5. Wait a minute. Why not the new–the new–

ACTOR 1. Earth? Uh, country, uh, world. That's it–the new world. *[ALL think about it]*

ALL. Not bad. / Sounds good. Etc.

SAM. *[Making a note on his clipboard]* Very well. The "new world" it is. Now let's get started. Okay? Everybody, go to Asia. It's offstage up there. Now when you get to Asia pretend to be an animal.

ACTOR 2. An animal?

ACTOR 4. Why should we be animals?

SAM. Because animals came to the new world before people did.

ACTOR 4. Okay, all you Asian animals–let's go! *[They exit upstage, ad-libbing the names of animals they wish to be. ACTOR 3 calls from offstage]*

ACTOR 3. What kind of animals were there, Sam?

SAM. According to my notes there were lots of different kinds. *[A drum cadence is heard offstage as the "ANIMALS" begin to cross Down Left and exit as they are announced]* Trumpeting elephants . . . fierce wolves . . . roaming buffaloes . . . proud peacocks . . . trotting camels . . . graceful tigers . . . galloping horses. *[The ANIMALS are gone]* We don't know who the first people to come here were, but it's almost certain that they were following the–

[A girl, AŜHA–pronounced AH-shah–and a boy, BALOE–pronounced BAY-low–enter hurriedly]

ASHA. Come, Baloe, we must catch at least one of the animals so it can take us back home.

BALOE. Slow down, Asha. We'll never catch them. They are too fast and too clever for us. We've chased them much too long already. That's why we are lost.

ASHA. Oh, Baloe. We are not lost. Home is right over there.

BALOE. No. It's in that direction.

ASHA. Are you sure?

BALOE. Yes. I mean–I think so. I mean–I don't know.

ASHA. Very well, silly. We'll go *my* way. *[They begin to walk]* Now there was this little strip of land. All we have to do is to retrace our steps and– *[They exit in different direction from which they came]*

SAM. Well, as you can see, those two children aren't going back the way they came. They *are* lost. Soon they'll find out that things are different here than back home in Asia. In the early days, Mother Nature was pretty ferocious here in the new world. There were volcanoes! *[Several ACTORS enter and create a "cone" with their outstretched arms. They make rumbling noises as they hoist aloft another ACTOR who holds a large folded red cloth. ASHA and BALOE enter and watch spellbound. The ACTOR leaps to the floor, unfurling the cloth which symbolizes molten lava. The others take hold of the "lava" and rush precariously close to ASHA and BALOE, who are frightened and jump out of the way. The "volcano" exits as the noise reaches a crescendo and subsides]* Glaciers! *[Two other ACTORS, holding a large white sheet, enter and chase ASHA and BALOE across the stage]* Icy glaciers! *[ASHA and BALOE stack up several cubes and crouch beneath them as the "glacier" exits]* Earthquakes! Mighty earthquakes! *[Several ACTORS enter quickly and crash into the cubes. They fall, narrowly missing Asha and Baloe. The ACTORS exit. ASHA is near tears]*

ASHA. Come, Baloe. We *must* find our way home! *[She takes his hand, and they exit]*

SAM. Despite the problems and difficulties here, it wasn't long till more people came to the new world.

ACTOR 2. *[Entering]* Sam, with all these dangers, why didn't the people just stay in Asia?

SAM. Different reasons I suppose. Some probably came looking for food.

ACTOR 1. *[Entering]* Hey, I just saw a big juicy woolly mammoth crossing the Bering Strait.

ACTOR 2. Big deal.

ACTOR 1. If we can catch him, we can have some barbecued woolly mammoth steaks.

ACTOR 2. Hey, that *is* a big deal. But hold the wool, will you?

SAM. Some came for new opportunities, I guess.

ACTOR 3. *[Entering with ACTOR 4]* Yep, this looks like a land of opportunity all right.

ACTOR 4. *[Not enthusiastic]* Yeah. With all these volcanoes and glaciers and earthquakes, you'll probably have the opportunity to get killed.

SAM. And others may have come—just because it was here.

ACTOR 5. *[Entering with ACTOR 6]* I don't know why you had to drag us to this place. What was wrong with Asia?

ACTOR 6. It was getting too crowded. Last year I must have seen ten or twelve people. I'm looking for an out-of-the-way place.

ACTOR 5. I think you just found it.

ACTOR 1. Hey, some of the ice and snow seems to be melting.

ACTOR 2. You're right. It's not quite as cold as it was.

ACTOR 3. It's not a bad neighborhood.

ACTOR 4. It may not be perfect. But it could be a lot worse.

ACTOR 6. Let's stay. *[ALL agree]*

ACTOR 1. Where will we live, Sam?

SAM. *[Looking at the clipboard]* It says here you'll dwell in caves for the first few thousand years.

ACTORS. *[Running to various cubes]* This is my cave. / I'll take this cave. / My cave is right here. Etc.

ACTOR 4. *[Tidying up a cube]* It takes a heap o' livin' to make a house a cave I always say.

ACTOR 3. *[With his "wife" as they talk to a "real estate salesman"]* This is a nice cave.

SALESMAN. You won't find a better cave anywhere. The price is rock bottom. Get it? Uh, you're no more than a stone's throw from anything. Get it—stone's throw? Uh, just look at this cave—don't take it for granite. Get it—don't take it for *granite.*

ACTOR 3. *[Not impressed by the jokes]* We'll buy it.

SALESMAN. *[Shaking hands with him]* Thank you—thank you. *[To the audience]* Works everytime. When I hit 'em with my jokes, they just —cave in. Get it? Cave in!

ALL. We got it. *[The ACTORS are now settled into their caves. ASHA enters with BALOE]*

ASHA. Baloe, look. People! *[They go to a "cave" and knock]*

ACTOR 1. Who is it?

ACTOR 2. Probably the Welcome Wagon. They're everywhere, you know. *[Going to the "door" and seeing the children]* Oh, hello.

ASHA. We're terribly sorry to bother you, but—

BALOE. We're lost.

ACTOR 2. Where did you come from?

ASHA. Asia.

ACTOR 2. So did we.

ASHA. Then you must know the way back home.

ACTOR 2. Sure. It's that way–or maybe it's–that way–gee, I seem to have forgotten. Maybe we can phone the Triple-A for directions. *[SAM shakes his head]* Oh, yeah. No phones . . . no Triple-A either. Look. Go north and turn left at the glacier. That oughta get you to the Bering Strait. After that, it's just a hop, skip, and slide back home.

ASHA. Thank you very much.

ACTOR 2. Say, even though we're almost out of food, here's a couple of sandwiches for your journey. *[She gives them the sandwiches]*

BALOE. Thank you. What kind of sandwiches are they?

ACTOR 2. Buffalo-burgers. S'long. *[ASHA and BALOE bid him good-bye and exit]* Boy, I hope those kids make it home okay. I also hope we can find something to eat around here. Sam, we're outta food. What do we do?

SAM. *[Looking at the clipboard]* According to my notes, people started moving around so they could find food. Some became hunters. *[Two or more ACTORS become hunters]*

HUNTERS. That's us. / We'll be the hunters. Etc.

SAM. Others became fishers.

FISHERS. Come on. / Let's be fishers. Etc.

FISHER. You clean 'em, I'll cook 'em.

SAM. And the rest became food gatherers.

FOOD GATHERERS. *[Getting together]* Come on, food gatherers. / I'll gather nuts. / I'll gather berries–

FOOD GATHERER 1. And I'll gather cracker jacks and fruit loops and–

FOOD GATHERER 2. *[Hitting him with a basket]* You're nothing but a fruit loop yourself.

SAM. For a while, everyone was very happy.

HUNTERS (1st CAMP). The hunters.

FISHERS (2nd CAMP). The fishers.

FOOD GATHERERS (3rd CAMP). And the food gatherers.

ALL. All live together in peace . . . *[they sing a cappella and in harmony]* AND HAR-MO-NY!

FOOD GATHERER 1. We trade with each other.

HUNTER 1. Here is one skin.

FISHER 1. *[Taking the skin]* In exchange for one fish. *[He gives it to the hunter]*

FOOD GATHERER 2. In exchange for one measure of grain. *[He takes the skin and gives the grain to the Fisher]*

ALL. We live in peace . . . *[singing]* AND HAR-MO-NY! *[The camps separate slightly and engage in quiet activities]*

SAM. But before long, things were not so peaceful.

FOOD GATHERER 1. *[Approaching a hunter]* Excuse me.

HUNTER 1. Yaz?

FOOD GATHERER 1. Those buffalo you chased through here yesterday–

HUNTER 1. Yaz?

FOOD GATHERER 1. –destroyed my grain.

HUNTER 1. Yaz. Well, your grain shouldn't be in the path of the buffalo. *[The FOOD GATHERER angrily returns to his camp only to be confronted by a FISHER]*

FISHER 1. Pardon me.

FOOD GATHERER 1. Uh-huh?

FISHER 1. You know those reeds by the river that you make blankets with?

FOOD GATHERER 1. Uh-huh.

FISHER 1. Well, the fish need those reeds to spawn in.

FOOD GATHERER 1. To what in?

FISHER 1. To spawn in–to have children in. And children fish grow into big fish and that's what fishers eat.

FOOD GATHERER 1. Well, you should be grain-eaters like us. We need those reeds, so your fish can just find somewhere else to spawn. *[The FISHER angrily returns to his camp and mimes casting for fish. A HUNTER approaches]*

HUNTER 2. Hey, you.

FISHER 1. Yeah?

HUNTER 2. You fishers are always fishing at the biggest fishing holes.

FISHER 1. That's the general idea.

HUNTER 2. Well, that's where the buffalo get their water. You scare them off.

FISHER 1. We wouldn't hurt a fly.

FISHER 2. Much less a buffalo.

HUNTER 2. *They* don't know that.

FISHER 2. Then tell 'em. We're not budging. Hey, I think I've got a bite.

HUNTER 2. You're gonna get a bite, all right.

FOOD GATHERERS. *[Joining them]* If there's any biting around here, we'll do it.

FISHER 2. *[As the others arrive]* Oh, yeah! *[They fight]*

SAM. Cut! *[They freeze]* There seems to be a little trouble here.

HUNTER 1. Just a–friendly disagreement. But we still live together...

ALL. *[Singing]* IN HAR-MO-NY! *[A HUNTER steps on the foot of a FISHER, who yells in pain and gouges a GATHERER. He winces and hits the HUNTER. Suddenly they are fighting again]*

SAM. Cut! I have a suggestion. Maybe you need a little vacation from each other. After all, you've been living together for several hundred years now.

ACTOR 1. We have?

ACTOR 2. They say time flies when you're having fun.

SAM. Let's try this and see how it works. You fishers go to the east–land of forests and streams. *[The FISHERS break camp, perhaps taking a cube or two with them and go to extreme Down Left]*

FISHERS. Bye, hunters; bye, food gatherers.

OTHERS. Yeah, so long.

SAM. Hunters to the Great Plains–land of wild animals.

HUNTERS. *[Heading toward Up Right Center]* See ya, food gatherers.

FOOD GATHERERS. Right, take it easy.

SAM. Food gatherers, to the west, south of the mountains where there is plenty of grain and seeds.

FOOD GATHERERS. *[As they start Down Right]* Bye, everybo–oh, yeah, there's nobody left. *[The new camps are assembled]*

FISHERS. Having–

HUNTERS. Wonderful–

FOOD GATHERERS. Time . . .

ALL. Wish you were here–

FISHER 2. Living in . . .

ALL. *[Singing, somewhat sadly]* HAR-MO-NY!

SAM. *[To the audience]* And that gives you a pretty good idea of how people became spread out all over the new world. *[Applauding the actors]* You played your parts very well, actors.

ACTORS. Thanks, Sam. / It was fun. Etc.

ACTOR 1. What comes next?

SAM. *[As they gather around the clipboard]* Hey, this looks like fun. Get ready now. *[The others agree and go to the trunks to get ready for the next segment]* First of all, we need a husband–

HUSBAND. Here.

SAM. His wife.

WIFE. Present.

SAM. And their children.

HUSBAND. Sorry. Uh, no children. *[ASHA and BALOE enter. They look about searchingly]*

WIFE. Who's that? Hansel and Gretel?

SAM. It's the children from Asia–Asha and Baloe. They must still be lost.

HUSBAND. Then we'll adopt them. At least for now. Hi, there. We need a couple of kids for this scene we're doing. Wanna join us?

ASHA. I–I suppose. We don't seem to be going anywhere.

BALOE. Except in circles. Can you show us how to get home?

HUSBAND. Sure. After the scene. Okay, Sam. We've got a wife, a husband, and two kids. What comes next?

SAM. We need a few animals about the countryside. *[Making animal sounds, the ANIMALS take their places]* Okay, action. *[To the audience]* "Action" means–begin.

HUSBAND. I have a terrific idea. Do you know what this cave needs?

WIFE. A good cleaning, I know.

HUSBAND. Huh-uh.

ASHA. A big swing out front.

HUSBAND. Nope.

BALOE. A tree house in the back? *[HUSBAND shakes his head]*

WIFE. What then?

HUSBAND. A pet.

WIFE. Very well, children, pet him. *[They do so]* And one from me– *[She pats him]*

HUSBAND. *[Laughing]* Thanks, but I don't mean *that* kind of pet– I mean an *animal* pet.

WIFE. But there's never been any such thing as an animal pet before.

HUSBAND. Then we'll be the first to have one.

ASHA. What kind of animal is this pet going to be?

HUSBAND. I don't know. *[They search about, stopping at the various animals who are grazing, sleeping, etc.]*

WIFE. How about a giraffe?

HUSBAND. Maybe–maybe so. Uh, giraffe–wanna be a pet? I say– how would you like to be a pet? *[Very loud]* I said–do you want to be our pet?

GIRAFFE. *[Finally acknowledging him]* I heard you the first time.

HUSBAND. Then why didn't you answer?

GIRAFFE. Giraffes cannot make sounds.

HUSBAND. Oh–well, why didn't you say so? *[The GIRAFFE mouths out front: "Giraffes–cannot–make–sounds"]* Oh, yeah–sure. Well, he probably wouldn't fit in the cave anyway.

WIFE. And if he ever got a sore throat, you'd never hear the last of it.

BALOE. How about this buffalo?

BUFFALO. *[Looking up]* Would you kindly refer to me as a bison.

BALOE. I'm sorry.

BUFFALO. Perfectly all right, but "bison" sounds so much more dignified than "buffalo," you know, and I need all the dignity I can muster.

HUSBAND. Of course.

WIFE. Mr. Bison, would you like to be a pet?

BUFFALO. Sorry, but I roam around a lot. I'd be hard to keep at home. Anyway, I'm awful tired. I just got back from a big celebration they had out east a few years ago.

HUSBAND. Yeah, what kind of celebration was it?

BUFFALO. They called it the Bison-tennial. Be seeing ya. *[He leaves]*

HUSBAND. He's friendly enough, all right, but I can't imagine him fetching my slippers. *[As they come to a sleeping member of the canine family]* I've got it–a wolf.

ASHA. Wolves are dangerous–

WIFE. Wolves are ferocious–

HUSBAND. Okay–wolves are out.

CANINE. *[Jumping up, rather fierce at first]* Wait a minute. Whadja call me?

HUSBAND. A wolf.

WIFE. Sir.

CANINE. *[Milder, but rather disgusted]* I am not now–nor have I ever been–nor will I become, even if nominated–a wolf.

HUSBAND. But you look like a wolf.

CANINE. And you look like a monkey, but I perceive you are not one.

WIFE. We are–distantly related to the monkey.

CANINE. And I am distantly related to the wolf. But the wolf is a canis lupus. *I* am a canis familiaris.

HUSBAND. You're a genuine canis familiaris?

CANINE. In the flesh–or, uh, in the fur as it were.

WIFE. Mr. Canis, can we call you something else?

CANINE. Canis is the only name I've got.

WIFE. Well, anyway, Mr. Canis, how would you like to be our pet?

CANINE. *[Suspiciously]* Uh-huh. And what's in it for me?

HUSBAND. Friendship.

WIFE. Companionship.

CANINE. I get it. I gotta jump through a hoop, learn how to shake hands, roll over and play dead–fetch, heel, stay, come, sit, stand, keep off the carpet and guard the cave–all for a little friendship–a little companionship. Huh-uh. Who needs it? I'm just fine right here, thanks.

WIFE. *[After a pause]* Mr. Canis–we'll feed you.

CANINE. Oh?

ASHA. We'll groom you.

CANINE. Yeah?

WIFE. We'll let you lie in front of the fire at night.

CANINE. Really?

HUSBAND. *[Imitating the animals as he mentions them]* Away from the lions and tigers–and *wolves!*

CANINE. Now stop that–you're scaring me.

BALOE. We'll pet you.

WIFE. We'll stroke you.

THE FAMILY. We'll love you. *[CANINE looks at one and then the other for a moment. Suddenly he bursts into tears]*

CANINE. You're too nice to me. I don't deserve you after the way I acted. I'm not good enough to be your pet. I was being selfish and greedy. I feel like–a *dog. [The FAMILY agrees to the name: "Hey, good name," / "I think that's it." Etc.]*

HUSBAND. That's what we'll call you–*dog*–if you will be our pet.

CANINE. Will I? I'll be the greatest pet ever. I'll be man's best friend –and woman's, too–shucks, I got no hang-ups about that.

WIFE. Dog–guess what? You're the first animal in the whole wide world to be domesticated.

CANINE. *[Swelling with pride]* You're kiddin'.

WIFE. Huh-uh.

CANINE. Me–domesticated. I can't believe it. I'm domesticated–officially and absolutely the world's first domesticated animal– *[Dropping at their feet and weeping]* You're too good to me.

WIFE. Now, now–

CANINE. *[Snapping out of it]* Say, what's "domesticated" mean anyway?

HUSBAND. It means to be tamed–

WIFE. To live in peace–

ASHA. With a family.

CANINE. *[Kissing their hands]* Thank you–bless you. *[Rising]* To think I hesitated to become domesticated. I was too shy to try the family way. But now that I'm tame, I'll never be the same, 'cause it's a dog's life today! *[The FAMILY applauds as CANINE bows]*

HUSBAND. Now, dog, your first duty is to help the kids find their way home. They want to go back to Asia.

CANINE. *[He sniffs around, then points]* It's thataway. *[ASHA and BALOE thank him and leave, waving good-bye to the family]* I know it's not nice to point, but I can't help it. I'm a–

ALL. Pointer! *[They laugh. SAM looks at the clipboard]*

SAM. Well, believe it or not, we've already spent several thousand years here in the new world. *[ALL express astonishment]* Not a lot went on during that time really. But before long, things started picking up.

ACTOR 1. Sam, how do people–scientists, I mean–know what really happened back then?

SAM. By examining old bones and hunting grounds and campsites.

ACTOR 2. But how do they know *when* the people–and the animals–were here?

SAM. Well, it's a little complicated, but they can do it. The method they use is called the radio-carbon analysis.

ACTOR 2. Radio-carbon–oh, they look at the caveman's radio and see what station he was listening to. *[The other ACTORS "pooh-pooh" the idea as SAM laughs]*

SAM. Everything has radio-active carbon in it. The newer something is, the more radio-active carbon it has. The older something is, the less it has. So, scientists can measure how much radio-active carbon a thing has in it–and tell how old it is.

ACTOR 2. You mean they could measure my radio-active carbon and know that I'm nineteen years old?

SAM. Probably. But I think it would be easier if they just looked at your birth certificate. *[ALL laugh]*

ACTOR 1. I feel sorry for the first people that were born.

ACTOR 2. Why?

ACTOR 1. They spent all their time huddled in caves, looking for food–or, if they were like poor Asha and Baloe–trying to find their way back home. They didn't have any fun.

SAM. Well, it's true they didn't go to movies or baseball games or roller rinks. But there is eviidence–

ACTOR 2. *[Smugly]* Through radio-carbon analysis?

SAM. Right.

ACTOR 2. I pick up things pretty quick.

ACTOR 1. *[Picking up ACTOR 2 and whirling her around] I* pick up things pretty quick, too. *[ALL laugh]*

ACTOR 2. Hey, stop it. Put me down! *[ACTOR 1 does so]*

SAM. There is evidence that early man did have a *few* forms of recreation. And one of the favorites was–the buffalo hunt. *[The ACTORS excitedly prepare for the hunt. Some drape fur pieces over their shoulders, while others take up spears]* The main thing to remember is to kill only those buffalo that you will eat.

HUNTER 1. Why else would we kill them?

SAM. For skins–or worse–for sport.

HUNTER 1. What do you mean–for sport?

SAM. It means for the pleasure of the hunters.

HUNTER 2. We wouldn't do anything selfish like that.

SAM. Okay. All set? Let the hunt begin.

[The stalking and charges of the HUNTERS are off-set by the parrying and escapes of the BUFFALO. Using the cubes as sighting ledges, hiding places, etc., the hunter and hunted perform a ritualistic ballet to the beat of drums and/or other rhythmic instruments. Finally, the BUFFALO are driven upstage–or behind the screens, if used–as the HUNTERS' voices climax the success of the hunt. Moments later, the HUNTERS emerge joyously displaying the furs]

SAM. You killed lots of buffalo today.

HUNTER 1. Oh, yes.

SAM. You have their skins, but where is the meat?

HUNTER 2. We already have enough meat. Today we killed only for skins.

HUNTER 3. And sport.

SAM. Don't you worry about destroying too many buffalo?

HUNTER 1. But they are so plentiful. Look, they dot the plains like a million lava rocks.

SAM. Still, don't you think you should protect them?

HUNTER 2. There'll be plenty of buffalo, no matter how many we kill.

HUNTER 3. Sure, who else could destroy them besides us?

HUNTER 1. No one–

HUNTER 2. Nothing at all– *[A TSE-TSE FLY peeks around a screen]*

FLY 1. Except– *[TSE-TSE FLY 2 appears from behind a screen]*

FLIES. Us.

HUNTER 2. You?

HUNTER 3. *[Laughing]* Who are you?

FLY 2. The tse-tse flies.

HUNTER 1. Tse-tse flies? You can destroy the buffalo? *[The HUNTERS laugh]*

FLIES. *[They are interesting, in a strange sort of way]* Never underestimate the tse-tse fly. When we come around the party starts to die! *[With their hands they put a "hex" out Right]*

HUNTER 2. *[As the HUNTERS view in amazement]* Look–those buffalo–they fell down.

FLIES. Buzzin' and a-bitin' is our claim to fame. Gettin' rid of animals is our game! *[Again the "hex"–this time out Center]*

HUNTER 3. Over there–those buffalo–they're–they're–

FLIES. With our little stingers we strike quite a blow. 'Specially when we start to sting the buffalo! *[They "hex" out Left]*

HUNTER 1. Those poor animals–they're–all–dead.

FLIES. *[Leaving]* Never underestimate the tse-tse fly. When we come around the party starts to die! *[They disappear behind the screens]*

SAM. So, the buffalo disappeared from the land for the next several hundred years. We're not sure if the tse-tse fly caused it. There aren't any tse-tse flies in America today. But several species of that insect have been found in rock strata here. Anyway, whatever happened, a part of the blame goes to the hunters who weren't willing to conserve what they had. *[The ACTORS sadly nod their heads]* Okay, okay–I think we all know it was a big mistake to kill the buffalo for sport, but we can't let it get us down. Go back to work now–this new world isn't going to run itself, you know.

ACTOR 1. Right, Sam.

ACTOR 2. What comes next?

SAM. One of the most important discoveries since man arrived in the new world.

ACTOR 3. The automobile? *[ALL admonish him]*

ACTOR 4. The airplane? *[He is razzed]*

ACTOR 5. I know–the frisbee. *[ALL playfully hit him]*

SAM. No, the automobile, the airplane, *and* the frisbee are still a long way off.

ACTOR 1. *[Coming down, holding a cornstalk]* I think I've got it. The new discovery is–farming!

SAM. Right! *[The others are not overly impressed]* Well, think about it. After nearly 10,000 years of hunting and fishing and searching for grain, you can now grow food in your own back yard.

ACTOR 2. Hey, I hadn't thought of that before. *[ALL begin to agree that farming isn't a bad discovery after all]*

ACTOR 3. *[To the actor with the cornstalk]* What else have you got in your garden?

ACTOR 1. Go see for yourself. *[Three ACTORS rush upstage and bring down the new crops]*

ACTOR 4. Corn!

ACTOR 5. Beans!

ACTOR 6. Squash!

SAM. And those were the first crops in the new world. Soon there were others.

ACTOR 1. Melons. *[A cheer]*

ACTOR 2. Millet. *[A cheer]*

ACTOR 3. Gourds. *[A cheer]*

ACTOR 4. Sweeeeet potatoes!

[They divide into three groups and begin to mime farming. The first group begins the following song to the tune of "Row, Row, Row Your Boat." After it has been sung through once, the second group picks up the "round," followed, then, by the third group]

ALL. GROW, GROW, GROW YOUR CROP,
HOEING AS YOU GO,
PLANTING IT, WATERING IT,
DIGGING IT UP,
REAPING WHAT YOU SOW! *[As the singing fades, a new crop is discovered]*

ACTOR 1. Hey, look here! This is the best crop of all.

ALL. What is it? / What does he have? Etc.

ACTOR 1. *[Producing a tobacco leaf]* Tobacco!

ACTOR 2. What's tobacco?

ACTOR 3. Is it good? *[Tasting it]* P-too-ie!

ACTOR 1. Wait–wait–you don't eat it. You *smoke* it.

ACTOR 4. *[Incredulously]* Smoke it?

ACTOR 1. Sure–you put it in a little pipe. *[He puts a few pieces of tobacco into the already packed pipe]*

ACTOR 2. Uh, what's a pipe?

ACTOR 1. I just invented it.

ACTOR 3. Why?

ACTOR 1. *[A bit impatiently]* What good's tobacco without a pipe?

ACTOR 3. Oh.

ACTOR 1. Okay, anybody got a light?

ACTOR 4. Sure–here's a piece of flint and steel.

ACTOR 2. Say, that's a nice flint and steel.

ACTOR 4. Got it for my birthday–initials right there.

ACTOR 1. Okay, here goes! *[ACTOR 4 "lights" the pipe as he strikes the steel to the flint and ignites a match hidden in the apparatus. ACTOR 1 puffs the pipe as the others watch in amazement. (NOTE: the "smoking" may be real or mimed)]*

OTHERS. Wow, look at that! / Looks like a little volcano! Etc.

ACTOR 5. How is it?

ACTOR 1. *[After a long, suffocating series of coughs]* Great!

ACTOR 2. Can I try it?

OTHERS. *[Getting in line]* Me too! / Pass it down! Etc. *[ACTOR 2 takes a puff and passes it. Each ACTOR coughs loudly and praises the pipe]* Terrific. / Marvelous. / The greatest. Etc.

ACTOR 3. Let's hear it for tobacco!

ALL. Hip-hip, cough-cough! Hip-hip, cough-cough! Hip-hip, cough-cough! *[They run behind the screens, or upstage, as they continue to cough until they are gone]*

SAM. Along with farming came other discoveries in the new world. They may not seem like much today, but back then they were very important. *[ACTORS return (or new group enters)]*

ACTOR 1. *[Holding up a crude stone tool]* Look, I've shaped this rock into a garden tool. I can dig with it, and hammer with it, and–

ACTOR 2. Say, can I borrow that new tool? *[She takes it and exits]*

ACTOR 1. –and lend it to my neighbor.

ACTOR 3. *[Holding a pot]* Look at this. Look at this! I discovered a pot!

ACTOR 4. Hey, neat trick. How'd you do that?

ACTOR 3. Well, I took a basket, see—and smoothed some clay around it so the basket would hold water.

ACTOR 4. Yeah?

ACTOR 3. I put it down next to the fireplace.

ACTOR 4. Oh, no.

ACTOR 3. I set it too close to the fire.

ACTOR 4. Oh, no.

ACTOR 3. The basket burned up.

ACTOR 4. Oh, no.

ACTOR 3. But it also dried out the clay. And now I've got—

ACTOR 4. A pot!

ACTOR 3. Right. I can put tools in it. I can put flowers in it. I can gather food in it—

ACTOR 4. Yes, but there's a better use than that for a pot.

ACTOR 3. Oh?

ACTOR 4. You can put it on your head and wear it to parties. *[He does so and goes dancing away]*

ACTOR 3. Maybe when somebody invents a lampshade, I can get my pot back. *[ALL laugh]*

SAM. Farming, new tools, new vessels—yep, everything was going pretty well after 10,000 years. *[ASHA and BALOE enter]*

ACTOR. *[He was the "Husband" earlier]* Look, it's Asha and Baloe. What are you kids doing here?

ASHA. We can't get back home.

HUSBAND. You're lost again?

BALOE. We finally found the path, but—

BOTH. It melted.

HUSBAND. Melted? The Bering Strait melted?

ASHA. It's nothing but water now.

HUSBAND. That must mean the ice age is over. Sam, can't we build a boat for them?

SAM. Boats were unknown back then. At least in the new world.

HUSBAND. Maybe they could swim.

SAM. It's fifty-six miles across the Bering Strait.

HUSBAND. Maybe they could float over in innertubes. Oh, yeah. No cars, no tires, no innertubes.

ASHA. It's okay. Maybe we can't go home again. But at least we have each other. *[She and BALOE embrace]*

HUSBAND. And you have us.

ASHA. You?

HUSBAND. Sure. We'll be your friends. We'll all stick together. We'll be as thick as thieves. *[The ACTORS, ASHA, and BALOE all embrace delightedly as two ROBBERS enter, laughing to themselves]*

ROBBER 2. Did you hear that, Robber Number One? Thick as *thieves,* they said.

ROBBER 1. Indeed I did hear it, Robber Number Two.

ROBBER 2. You know, these people in the new world have got lots of nice things, Robber Number One.

ROBBER 1. Right, Robber Number Two. I'd like some of those things myself. Let's attack 'em, and head for the border, y'hear.

ROBBER 2. Sounds good to me.

ROBBER 1. There is one little bitty problem though. There's more of them than us.

ROBBER 2. Then I'll just *de*-vide and conquer.

ROBBER 1. How do you do that?

ROBBER 2. You mean you graduated from Robber School and you don't know how to *de*-vide and conquer?

ROBBER 1. I musta been sick the day they covered that. *[The other ACTORS are talking among themselves]*

ROBBER 2. Well, just watch me, and you'll get the general idea. *[He quietly takes ASHA and a few ACTORS aside, unknown to the others]* Hi there. How are y'all? Why do you associate with those other people?

ASHA. They're our friends.

ROBBER 2. Oh, you're much too good for them–nicer looking– *[ROBBER 1 has caught on and is ushering BALOE and several others Down Right as he mimes telling them the same thing as Robber 2]* Whiter teeth–you're just plum handsomer and much smarter.

ASHA. You think so?

ROBBER 2. Have I ever lied to you before?

ASHA. Well, no, but–

ROBBER 2. There, you see. Now y'all jest get up on this here pedestal where you belong. *[He hoists Asha onto a cube Down Left and hands her a small pennant on a stick. Approximately the same action is happening Down Right with Baloe receiving a pennant of another color]*

REMAINING ACTORS. *[In a third "camp"]* Well, how do you like that? They left us alone like we were trash. We'll show them! *[One of them stands on a Down Center cube as ROBBER 2 hands him a pennant]*

STAGE LEFT ACTORS. Hoo-ray for our side! We are the best! Yes—we are the best, yes!

STAGE CENTER ACTORS. Our side's better than your side! Our side's better than yours!

STAGE RIGHT ACTORS. We're number one, hey! We're number one, hey! We're number one!

ALL. *[Each group mocking the other]* Na-na-na-na-na-na—

[They repeat their taunts as the ROBBERS go to the Down Left actors and mime hitting them over the heads. They stretch the actors out beside the cube and "lift" an item or two from their pockets. The taunts continue from the other two groups who are oblivious to the Down Left action. The ROBBERS repeat the "mugging" at Down Center and finally at Down Right. Suddenly, it is silent]

ROBBER 2. Robber Number One, we have jest pulled off what they call in Robber School a *de*-vide and conquer.

ROBBER 1. You're a mighty fine teacher, Robber Number Two.

ROBBER 2. Let's be a-headin' south of the border. Soon as these "smart, handsome" folks get some more loot, we'll come again. Y'hear? *[They leave laughing. SAM rushes to the "victims" and helps them up]*

SAM. Hey, get up! They said they'd be back. And now that more people are learning about the new world, there'll be others who'll come and try to take what's yours.

BALOE. *[Dejectedly]* How can we stop them?

SAM. *[Reading oratorically from the clipboard]* "You can begin by sacrificing false pride in order to unite for the common good."

ALL. Huh? / What does that mean? Etc.

SAM. Yeah, I'm not sure I understood that myself. Look, let's try this— *[He gathers them Down Center and whispers instructions to them. He takes the small pennants from them and hands them a single large one]* Now remember what I told you. *[He leaves the action as the ROBBERS return]*

ROBBER 2. Okay, Robber Number One, let's git 'em again. *[The two split and go to the cubes at Down Right and Down Left respectively]*

ROBBER 1. Right, Robber Number Two. While they're still *de*-vided, we'll do some more conquerin'.

ROBBER 2. You larning fast, boy.

ROBBER 1. Hey, where they at?

ROBBER 2. They ain't here. They must be– *[They have moved to the front of the Down Center group without seeing them]*

ACTORS. Here!

ROBBER 2. Well, howdy now. What ch'all doin' together there? Why, you should be up on your different pedestals! *[They try to separate the actors without success]*

ACTORS. *[Waving the pennant, they loom large]* *We* are number one!

ROBBER 1. They seem serious.

ROBBER 2. I reckon.

ROBBER 1. What do we do now?

ROBBER 2. I don't know. I musta been sick when they covered this in Robber School. *[The ACTORS move toward the trembling ROBBERS. They catch the robbers, take from them the previously stolen items, tie their hands, and march them away behind the screens, shouting "We're number one"]*

SAM. It's hard to believe that it took almost 15,000 years for people just to get settled into the new world–deciding where to live, making a few discoveries and learning how to protect themselves. But in other parts of the planet, some very interesting things were happening. If there had been television back then, people here would have known what was going on elsewhere.

[Two ACTORS enter holding a large frame representing a TV screen. A NEWSCASTER and a CHINAMAN appear in the "screen." The other ACTORS form an audience in front of the TV]

NEWSCASTER. Good evening. This is Walter Crankcase with a news flash from one of the three great centers of the world. We have just learned that rice has been discovered in China.

CHINAMAN. The year 6,000–or so–B. C. will go down in history as a good year for the Chinese. There is no end to the many uses of our new crop–rice. Boiled rice, fried rice, rice pudding, rice cream–get it, rice cream? You eat it in a rice cream cone. *[The other ACTORS boo]* What an audience–but I got a million of 'em, folks. Did I tell you we're working on a new instrument–the compass. It's a magnet that points to the north. Only one thing wrong with it–take a guess.

ALL. *[Without enthusiasm]* It's not polite to point. *[He laughs as the other ACTORS yawn]*

CHINAMAN. Am I keeping you people awake? Okay, this is my last one. We're building a great wall around China to protect us from our enemies. Now if somebody would just invent paper, we'd cover our great wall with it. Know what we'd call this invention?

ACTOR. We can't imagine.

CHINAMAN. Wallpaper! *[He is in hysterics as the OTHERS groan and throw rice at him. An ACTOR with a hook reaches through the curtains and pulls the Chinaman offstage]* That was funny, I tell you. Where's your sense of humor? What a joint. Etc.

NEWSCASTER. Tune in again for more up-to-the-minute reports from the great centers of the world. *[The other ACTORS applaud and laugh. The CHINAMAN and the "HOOKER" rejoin the others who carry on a mock conversation among themselves. An ACTOR crosses to Sam]*

ACTOR 1. Boy, things were really up-to-date in China. Imagine that great wall! Why didn't people here have things like that, Sam?

SAM. Things happened here soon enough, but at that time folks were just too busy getting acquainted with their new world. Lots of people were still moving their homes from place to place. Here, I'll show you. I need a group here. *[He brings several ACTORS Down Left]* And another group here. *[He herds the remaining ACTORS–except one–Down Right]*

ACTOR 1. Hey, Sam, what about me?

SAM. *[Showing him the clipboard]* You will play this part.

ACTOR 1. Hey, that looks like fun.

SAM. You'll see. Action! *[He leaves the area. ACTOR 1 speaks to the audience]*

ACTOR 1. Hey, I think I'll start a rumor. I just love to start rumors. Now don't tell me rumors are bad. They're not bad. They're just–a little naughty. And such fun–the way they upset people and all. *[He goes to the Down Left group (Group 1)]* Say, people, have I got something to tell you. *[He whispers to them. They are shocked at his words]*

GROUP 1. What? / They wouldn't. / They couldn't. / *[Pause. In unison]* They might.

ACTOR 1. Oh yes, I heard it with my own ears. And I never tell lies. *[Sotto voce, to the audience]* Just rumors–hee, hee, hee.

GROUP 1 MEMBER. You heard those people over there say they were going to attack us–and steal from us?

ACTOR 1. No joshin'. *[He shows the audience his crossed fingers]*

GROUP 1 MEMBER. Listen everybody–emergency meeting. *[They huddle in deep discussion]*

ACTOR 1. *[Crossing to Group 2 at Down Right]* Say, people, wait till you get a load of this. *[He whispers to them]*

GROUP 2. What? / They wouldn't. / They couldn't. / *[Pause. In unison]* They might.

ACTOR 1. Oh, yes. I heard it with my own ears, and I never tell lies. *[To the audience]* Just rumors–hee, hee, hee.

GROUP 2 MEMBER. You heard those people over there say they were going to attack us and steal from us?

ACTOR 1. No joshin'.

GROUP 2 MEMBER. Hey–important meeting everybody. *[As they huddle, GROUP 1 disbands]*

GROUP 1 MEMBER. All right, it is agreed. We'll build our homes in those cliffs–way up there. That will protect us.

GROUP 1. Right. / To the cliffs! *[They begin to push cubes together and climb onto them as GROUP 2 breaks its huddle]*

GROUP 2 MEMBER. It is unanimous. We'll build our homes on those high hills with the flat tops.

GROUP 2. The mesas. / We'll move to the mesas! *[They also assemble cubes and climb onto them]*

ACTOR 1. Isn't this exciting? All this activity because of my little rumor. Hee, hee, hee, hee.

GROUP 1 MEMBER. There–we are now settled in the cliffs.

GROUP 2 MEMBER. At last–we are safe on the mesas.

GROUP 1 MEMBER. Hey, mesa people–you can't attack us now.

GROUP 2 MEMBER. Right, cliff dwellers–and you can't steal from us either.

GROUP 1 MEMBERS. We know. *[A beat]*

BOTH GROUPS. Wait a minute!

GROUP 2 MEMBER. We never planned to attack you in the first place.

GROUP 1 MEMBER. And who said we wanted to steal from you? *[They turn and stare from their perches at ACTOR 1]*

ACTOR 1. It's just the little old rumor-maker me–hee, hee, hee. *[A pause]* Okay everybody–come on down. The game's over. *[Pause]* You'll have to admit it was a pretty good joke. Ha, ha. *[Pause]* Oh, come on down now. The rumor is finished. I–I'm getting a little lonesome down here.

GROUP 1 MEMBER A. You know, the air certainly is clean up here. Maybe we should stay in the cliffs.

GROUP 2 MEMBER A. And the view is so nice from up here, perhaps we should remain on the mesa.

GROUP 1 MEMBER B. Staying here will protect us from invaders–

GROUP 2 MEMBER B. And from wild animals.

GROUP 1 MEMBER A. And now that the glaciers are starting to melt up north–

GROUP 2 MEMBER A. It'll protect us from–

ALL. Floods! *[With a rush, two ACTORS make a whooshing noise as they grab a large blue cloth and engulf ACTOR 1]*

ACTOR 1. Help! Glub-glub. I'll never start a rumor again. Glub-glub. No joshin'. Glub-glub.

[He is carried behind the screens. If desired, ACTOR 1 may flail about as though he is swimming off and a line can be added such as "He'll be swimming for a long, long while, so he'll have no time to start any more rumors." They laugh and shake hands with each other. ALL except ASHA and BALOE may exit]

SAM. So, Asha and Baloe. How do you like it here, so far?

ASHA. Fine, except–

SAM. Except what?

ASHA. It would be nice to–have somewhere to live.

BALOE. Yeah, to settle down with some people since we'll never be able to go back home.

SAM. Very well, you have several groups to choose from. North of here in the colder climate is a group who will be called the Eskimos. In the East where the forests lie is a tribe of people that will be named the Iroquois. And right here in the Southwest are the cliff dwellers who will be known as the Pueblos.

ASHA. I'm tired of traveling. I think I'd rather stay right here.

BALOE. Me, too. Anyway, it might be fun living way up on the side of a cliff.

SAM. Then cliff dwellers you shall be. *[ASHA and BALOE cheer and exit as SAM calls to them]* Just don't get too near the edge! I hope they keep in touch. Of course, without telephones and post offices, that might be kind of hard. *[A pause]* Speaking of keeping in touch, though, I wonder what's happening in the second great world center right now.

[ACTORS quickly set up the TV screen as the NEWSCASTER and two pushy yet likeable SALESMEN appear]

NEWSCASTER. Hello, again. Walter Crankcase here with a special report from Egypt, 2,000 B. C.

SALESMAN 1. Hey out there–we're the Nefertiti Brothers, and have we got an invention for you.

SALESMAN 2. The calendar!

SALESMAN 1. Building all those pyramids was hard work for the Egyptians.

SALESMAN 2. And after a week of hard work–you need a week-end to rest up.

SALESMAN 1. But if you don't have a calendar–

SALESMAN 2. How do you know when you come to week-ends–

SALESMAN 1. Or birthdays–

SALESMAN 2. Or holidays–

SALESMAN 1. Or most important–

BOTH. Summer vacations!

SALESMAN 2. If it weren't for the calendar, you'd probably have to go to school all year.

SALESMAN 1. So make a date to get your calendar today.

SALESMAN 2. And say–while we've got your attention, may we remind you of our newest invention–

SALESMAN 1. Bricks!

SALESMAN 2. And another handy item–

SALESMAN 1. Glass!

SALESMAN 2. And our greatest product–

SALESMAN 1. Mathematics!

SALESMAN 2. So, as sure as two and two equal five– *[Quickly, SALESMAN 1 whispers to him]* Uh, four–your number one stop for the best shopping anywhere is the Nefertiti Brothers way down in Egypt land.

SALESMAN 1. And say, while you're in the neighborhood, stop in and see our pyramids along the Nile.

SALESMAN 2. Hey, I think there's a song in that.

BOTH. Tut-tut. *[They disappear behind the curtain to applause]*

ACTOR 1. Hey, Walter Crankcase said it was 2,000 B. C. We're rolling right along. We may not be as advanced as China or Egypt, but everyone's happy here in the new world. We get along together pretty well.

SAM. We just have to make sure it stays that way.

ACTOR 1. Oh, it will. What could happen? I mean, we learned from the buffalo to take care of what we have. We learned from the robbers to take care of ourselves–

SAM. But you also need to learn to take care of each other.
ACTOR 1. What do you mean?
SAM. Watch.

[A BLUE-EYED person is approached by a GREEN-EYED person]

GREEN EYE 1. Your eyes are blue.
BLUE EYE. That's right.
GREEN EYE 1. All people whose eyes are blue will serve us people who have green eyes.
BLUE EYE. Are you sure?
GREEN EYE 1. You know it, blue. *[Grabbing Blue Eye]* Get me a pillow–get me a drink–get me a– *[BLUE EYE mimes serving Green Eye. Elsewhere, GRAY EYE approaches BROWN EYE, who is gardening]*
GRAY EYE. Hi, Brown Eye.
BROWN EYE. Oh, hello, Gray Eye.
GRAY EYE. Say, have you noticed what the Green Eyes are doing?
BROWN EYE. Oh, I heard about it, I guess.
GRAY EYE. Don't you think it's wrong?
BROWN EYE. *C'est la vie.*
GRAY EYE. You mean you're not going to do anything about it?
BROWN EYE. Look–I'm not going to get involved. My eyes are brown. I don't like what the Green Eyes are doing, and I feel sorry for the Blue Eyes–but I got my own problems.
GREEN EYE 2. *[Reading from a document]* It has just been decreed that all Brown Eyes, as well as Blue Eyes, will serve Green Eyes. *[Brown Eye is carried off]*
BROWN EYE. Now–now–wait a minute. I'm going to fight this! Call a meeting–help!
SAM. *[Running down to Brown Eye]* It's too late. You should have done something sooner–you should have seen your neighbor's danger as your own. *[ALL break the "act"]*
ACTOR 1. Don't worry, Sam. We wouldn't let something like that happen in the new world. Can you imagine anything sillier than some people thinking they're better than others because of the color of their eyes? *[ALL, except SAM, laugh]*
ACTOR 2. Or their hair? *[More laughter]*
ACTOR 3. Or their skin? *[Laughter begins, then quickly subsides when they realize what has been said]*

ACTOR 4. I think we need to talk this over.

ACTORS. Right. / I agree. Etc. *[They exit, talking among themselves]*

SAM. Life sure is nice. But it does get complicated every once in a while. *[A pause]* Say, I wonder how our two friends, Asha and Baloe, are doing in their new home. Maybe we can look in on them. *[ASHA and BALOE enter unsteadily with pots on their heads]* Asha, Baloe—what are you doing there?

ASHA. We're trying to bring water up to the village the way the Pueblos do. *[Two or three ACTORS deftly cross the stage carrying pots on their heads]* See?

POT-CARRIER. It's all in the head. *[The POT-CARRIERS exit]*

SAM. I'm sure you'll learn how before long. What else do the Pueblos do?

BALOE. Well, they've discovered a new plant called cotton, and they make clothes out of it. *[Two ACTORS cross the stage weaving cotton into cloth. ACTOR 1 starts racing ahead]*

ACTOR 2. Slow down just a cotton-pickin' minute, will ya? *[They exit]*

ASHA. And we have artists who draw pictures on the sides of the walls of the cliffs. *[Two or three ACTORS enter, carrying a large sheet of brown paper featuring "cave" drawings. An ARTIST is painting on the paper. They stop as ASHA, BALOE, and SAM examine it]*

SAM. Very interesting. I'm sure archaeologists will be happy to find these paintings someday.

ARTIST. Oh, this is nothing. Just depicting everyday life here in the cliffs. Quite dull if you ask me. I'm really more into sunsets and landscapes, but there's no money in that these days. *[He continues to paint as he exits with the ACTORS holding the paper]*

SAM. Pottery, weaving, art—pretty good, I'd say.

BALOE. But that's not the best part.

SAM. Then what is?

BALOE. The dances! They have dances for everything. *[Several DANCERS enter. ASHA and BALOE join them]* The Eagle Dance which praises the powers of the sky and asks for their help. *[To a drum cadence, they perform an Eagle Dance]*

ASHA. The Corn Dance—to pray for good crops and bountiful harvests. *[They perform a Corn Dance]*

BALOE. The Rain Dance—to ask for plenty of water for the soil, the animals, and the people. *[They perform a Rain Dance. Thunder is heard. Several ACTORS enter with umbrellas and exit with the DANCERS. ASHA calls to Sam]*

ASHA. Sometimes these dances really work.

SAM. Well, it looks as though Asha and Baloe are having a great time living with the Pueblos. *[A pause]* You know, we don't have a lot of time left, so I think we'd better hear from our third—and final—great world center.

[Again the ACTORS set up the TV screen as the NEWSCASTER and an EAST INDIAN appear. The other ACTORS become the audience]

NEWSCASTER. Walter Crankcase here reporting from India, where an important invention has just taken place in 900 B. C. In fact, you might say it's a very necessary invention.

EAST INDIAN. Thank you. Say, could anyone tell me where the bathroom is? *[He laughs, as does the ACTOR "audience"]* I know why you're laughing. You think there's no such thing as a bathroom. Well, you're wrong. Here in India we just invented the bathroom. We have pipes leading to and from our houses. Oh, we have other wonderful things, too. Like clothes made from fabrics—so much better than bark and animal hide—yuk—how tacky. And we also have tall buildings—some of them are six stories high—makes you dizzy just thinking about it. But my favorite invention is still the bathroom. *[Calling behind him]* Is my bubble bath ready? 'Bye now. Gotta go tidy up. *[Calling again]* Don't forget my toy sailboat and my rubber ducky. *[To the audience]* Oh, I just love the bathroom. You can see it if you like. But only one at a time. You have to stand in line. *[He exits. ALL laugh and chatter excitedly as they follow him off]*

NEWSCASTER. And that's the way it is. Goodnight, and have a good century. *[He exits]*

ACTOR 1. *[Entering with two or three other ACTORS]* Hey, Sam, what time is it?

SAM. *[Looking at his watch]* Looks like it's about—

ACTOR 1. No, no. I mean—what *year* is it?

SAM. Oh. *[Looking at his clipboard]* Almost 1,000 A. D.

ACTOR 2. Hey, it's nearly time for Christopher Columbus to arrive.

SAM. That's still a few years off.

ACTOR 3. But look! There's a ship right now. *[ACTORS who form a "Viking Ship" enter]*

SAM. It *is* a ship all right. But it doesn't belong to Columbus. *[The "ship" is slowly rowed Down Center. The "CREW" makes appropriate sound effects]*

ACTOR 3. Are they coming to attack us?

SAM. I don't think so. Go down to the shore and see who they are. *[The ACTORS do so. The VIKINGS "come ashore"]*

VIKING 1. Greetings.

ACTOR 3. Hello.

VIKING 1. We expected more people–more of a welcome than–this.

ACTOR 3. *[Puzzled]* I–I'm sorry, but–

VIKING 1. Where are your ships?

ACTOR 3. We have no ships.

VIKING 2. And where are your great feast halls?

ACTOR 2. Feast halls?

VIKING 2. For eating great feasts.

VIKING 3. Drinking great wines.

VIKING 4. And singing great songs of victories.

ALL VIKINGS. *[Except VIKING 1–singing]* HAIL TO THE VIKINGS! HAIL VICTORY!

VIKING 1. Quiet! I fear we shall be greatly disappointed here in Greenland.

ACTOR 1. Well, we don't have a lot, but–Greenland?

VIKING 1. Yes, Greenland.

ACTOR 1. Sir, I hate to tell you, but this is–the new world.

VIKING 1. There is no such place. *[Taking a map from VIKING 4]* Look. Last month we set sail from Iceland–here–*[referring to the map]* –headed for Greenland–here.

ACTOR 1. But you aren't here–*[pointing to the map]* –you're *here.*

VIKING 1. That's impossible. On this map, "here" is the middle of the ocean.

ACTOR 1. Then whoever made this map didn't know about the new world.

VIKING 1. Fellow sailors, let us examine this map.

VIKING 4. It wasn't my fault. *[They gather around the map]*

ACTOR 3. Sam, who are they?

SAM. Vikings–from the cold country.

ACTOR 3. They seem very advanced–I mean smart and everything.

SAM. They are advanced–but capable of sometimes getting lost. *[They laugh as the VIKINGS return]*

VIKING 1. It is obvious that somewhere we made a wrong turn–thanks to our navigator.

VIKING 4. It wasn't my fault.

VIKING 1. We shall again set sail. *[The VIKINGS return to the "ship"]*

ACTOR 2. Won't you stay?

VIKING 1. I'm afraid not. We were expected in Greenland last week.

VIKING 2. For the big feast.

ACTOR 3. Oh, yeah–wine and song and things.

VIKING 1. Yes. Sorry for the intrusion.

ACTOR 3. Oh, think nothing of it. It was nice to meet all you Vikings.

VIKING 1. Well, on to Greenland! *[To VIKING 4]* And this time, pay attention to the map. *[They are moving with appropriate sound effects]*

VIKING 4. I tell you, it wasn't my fault. *[They are gone]*

ACTOR 1. So, it was really the Vikings who discovered America, after all.

SAM. Well, they *were* here before Columbus, but they didn't officially discover it. *[A pause]* Time is sure moving along. Before you know it, we'll be welcoming Christopher Columbus himself– *[ASHA and BALOE enter]* Asha. Baloe. What are you doing here?

ASHA. The cliff dwellers are leaving.

SAM. Leaving? Why?

ASHA. There's been a terrible drought.

BALOE. There's no water any more. The crops won't grow. There's nothing to drink.

ASHA. I guess the Rain Dance stopped working.

SAM. Where are the cliff dwellers going?

BALOE. South, they said. They may even leave the new world.

SAM. Well, there are certainly other places here where you can live. As I mentioned, you can join the Eskimos, the Iroquois–and there are others–like these people. The Mound Builders of the midwest. *[Quietly, several ACTORS enter and begin to stack cubes Up Center]*

ASHA. What are they doing?

SAM. Constructing a large mound of earth.

BALOE. Why?

SAM. We've talked a lot about life here in the new world. But we haven't mentioned death.

ASHA. That's scary.

SAM. Not really. After all, death is also a part of life–a very natural part. *[A body–real or mimed–is borne behind the stack of cubes]* The Mound Builders are burying someone who has died. When they place him in the mound, it's a very special tribute. *[The ACTORS place objects–real or imagined–into the "mound"]*

ASHA. What are they doing now?

SAM. They're putting gifts into the mound–things to help their friend along in his next life.

BALOE. What kind of gifts?

ACTOR 1. The bow and arrows with which we hunted together.

ACTOR 2. A pair of moccasins to speed him on his journey.

ACTOR 3. A warm animal skin to keep him from being cold.

ASHA. *[Hesitatingly approaching them]* Excuse me. None of you seem to be crying. Aren't you sad?

ACTOR 3. We are sad that he is gone.

ACTOR 2. But because we were kind to him–

ACTOR 1. We know he was happy–

ALL. And that makes us glad.

ACTOR 1. When a person is happy in life, it is not as hard to see him go.

ACTOR 3. When it comes my time to rest in the mound, I hope my friends will say–

ACTORS. He was happy because of us.

ACTOR 3. And that will make me glad. *[They leave]*

ASHA. That's not a bad idea, Mound Builders.

BALOE. Not a bad idea at all. *[A pause]*

SAM. So, you can stay here, if you wish. Or you can move on to some of the other– *[Several ACTORS enter]*

ACTOR 1. Sam, guess what!

ACTOR 2. *[Pointing offstage]* Those Vikings left one of their smaller ships behind.

ACTOR 3. It's not in very good shape, but we could patch it up.

SAM. Why would you want to do that?

ACTOR 4. So that Asha and Baloe can sail across the Bering Strait and go back home to Asia–to be with their friends.

SAM. Hey, that's a good idea. What do you think, kids?

ASHA. That's awfully nice of you, but–well–you see–

BALOE. By now our friends are nearly 20,000 years old. We might not recognize them.

ASHA. And we like it so well here, we think we'll stay where we are.

If it's okay. *[ALL cheer. ASHA turns to Sam]* We heard you mention a Mr. Christopher Columbus. Who's he?

SAM. The man who will officially discover the new world.

BALOE. When is he coming?

SAM. Anytime now.

ASHA. Can we meet him?

SAM. Absolutely. Go look for three ships on the horizon.

BALOE. Great!

ASHA. 'Bye, everybody! Come on, Baloe. I wonder if Columbus will like it here as much as we do.

SAM. He'll probably be so happy when he gets here, he'll declare a national holiday.

BALOE. See you later, everybody. Wait for me, Asha! *[They leave as the ACTORS wave]*

ACTOR 1. I can't believe it. It's finally time for the discovery of America–at least, the *recent* discovery of America.

ACTOR 3. *Now* we can do the show we came to do in the first place.

ACTOR 2. I am Queen Isabella of Spain.

ACTOR 3. I am the captain of the great ship Pinta.

ACTOR 4. I'm a no-good sailor on the Santa–

SAM. I'm terribly sorry, everyone, but–well–I'm afraid the hour is gone.

ACTOR 4. It is?

ACTOR 1. I can't believe it.

ACTOR 2. It went so fast.

ACTOR 3. *[After a pause]* Well, let's pack up.

ACTOR 1. Yeah, time to hit the road again. *[They begin to gather the props and pack the trunks]*

ACTOR 3. You know? I think I had more fun doing the improvised play than the one we usually do. *[The OTHERS agree]*

ACTOR 1. Hey, I've got a great idea, Sam. Why don't you join us? We'll use your notes, and you can be in the play. *[ALL encourage him to do so]*

SAM. All right. I *will* join you. *[ALL applaud] But* you take the notes. *[He hands the clipboard to ACTOR 1]* And I'll stay backstage where the Stage Manager belongs.

ALL. Great. / Terrific. / I'm glad he's coming along. Etc. *[They continue packing their trunks, boxes, etc. SAM addresses the audience]*

SAM. Well, I guess things turned out pretty well after all. Oh, there's no question that Columbus's discovery of America was very important. But somehow, thinking about what happened here over the past 20,000 years is even more exciting. Think about it.

ACTORS. Okay. / All packed. / Let's go, Sam. Etc.

SAM. Wait a minute. You're forgetting a very important part of the theatre.

ALL. What? / I don't understand. Etc.

SAM. The curtain call!

ALL. Oh, yeah. / Sure. / How could we forget that? Etc. *[They line up Down Center]*

SAM. Wait a minute. Asha! Baloe! *[They enter]* Curtain call.

ASHA. Okay, but hurry up.

BALOE. We don't want to miss Columbus.

SAM. Actors, we salute you for a job well done. *[He leads the applause as the ACTORS bow. ALL exit with their trunks, boxes, etc.]* I'll join you in a minute. *[To the audience]* It's not often that the Stage Manager gets to visit with the audience. And even though I do belong backstage, I had a lot of fun this morning (afternoon or evening). Hope you did, too. Have a good day. *[He bows and exits]*

The End

PRODUCTION NOTES

Properties

Clipboard—Sam

All the following props are loaded in boxes or trunks:

Large folded red cloth (molten lava)
Large white sheet (glacier)
Sandwiches
Animal skins
Fish
Bag or basket of grain
} may be mimed
Spears
Pieces of fur cloth (buffalo hides)
Cornstalk
Raw vegetables (beans, squash, lettuce, etc.)
Tobacco leaf (or can of pipe tobacco)
Tobacco pipe
Flint and steel (rock and small piece of metal, with a concealed match)
Stone tool (a sharp-pointed stone, or papier mache tomahawk)
Several pots (of unbreakable material painted to look like clay, perhaps with pre-Columbian designs)
3 small pennants
1 large pennant
Large frame symbolizing a TV screen
Rice
Large hook (like a shepherd's crook)
Large blue cloth (flood)
Skeins of string (for weaving)
Large sheet of brown paper with primitive drawings
Paint brush
Several umbrellas
Map
Bow and arrow
Moccasins
Animal skin
} for Mound Builders—may be mimed

Costumes and Make-up

A simple basic costume, as suggested in the "Notes on the Play" (page 4), is recommended. The various characters and animals can be suggested with a simple addition—headpiece, cape, shawl, coat, fur cloth, animal ears, and so on. The basic make-up should also be simple. Additional make-up, such as animal whiskers, large eyes, etc., may be added to symbolize a certain animal or type of person. However, the play must not stop or slow down for costume or make-up changes. Posture, gesture, and pantomime can be as effective as costume and make-up for indicating character, including animals.

Special Effects

No special lighting or sound effects are called for, although the director is at liberty to use whatever technical equipment is available. Lighting and background music fitting the mood of each scene are possibilities as long as they do not take focus away from the actors. To keep young audiences entertained, the play must be lively and fast-moving.

The dances can be improvised—perhaps spread-eagle arms flying through the clouds for the eagle dance, corn stalks rising out of the ground (actors stooping and then rising, and then raising their arms as the leaves grow) for the corn dance, and stomping, running, and hopping with arms thrusting heavenward for the rain dance. Children are especially adept at improvising dances of this type.

Floor Plan

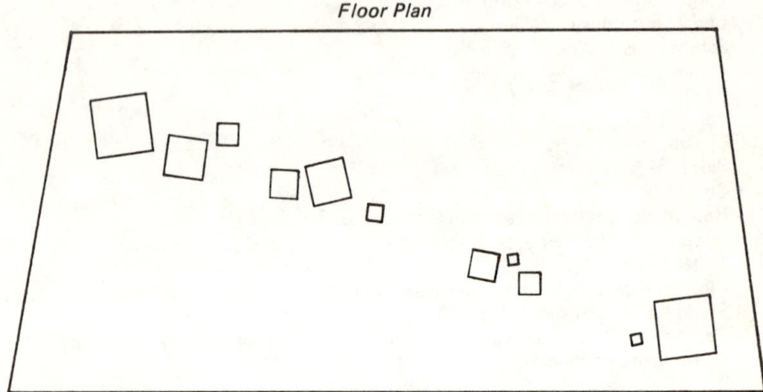

Several cubes of varying sizes scattered about the stage provide the only set pieces needed. These should be sturdy enough to support actors standing on them, yet light enough to move around and stack easily. One side of at least some of the cubes should be open so that they can serve as caves.

If the play is presented in a room or out of doors, several folding screens may be placed upstage so that actors not appearing in a scene may disappear behind them. Actors can also form a live backdrop by standing in a line upstage with their backs to the audience, turning in whenever they appear in a scene. On a proscenium stage, actors may, of course, exit into the wings.

Comments—for use in your publicity releases (continued from page 4)

bill. Very small children may not have fully grasped the history/plot of the show, but the quick action & bright colors kept them with us. Middle graders...enjoyed the crazy puns, the silly historical/hysterical suggestions of the cast members... & certainly the show's quick pace kept their interest. And...our largely adult audience let down those 'adult defenses' & laughed good & heartily at the humor they found at every turn...I was so very pleased with the show—the script, the performances, the company, the applause."—Sue Molden, Appleton H. S. West

"Students and teachers alike are enthusiastic about ***A*B*C******."**—Jo Anne M. Uzel, Theatre Specialist, Maryland-National Capital Park & Planning Commission

"Always exciting, often moving. The adults enjoyed it as much as the children—the show had something for everyone. A totally unique script that kept the actors enthusiastic from opening rehearsal to final curtain."—Rita Keller, Director, Delaware County Community College

"The UW-Whitewater Commedia Players and I are enjoying the marvelous opportunities which ***A*B*C**** **provides for actors to adapt the script to their talents. [My actors'] ages range from fifteen to twenty-six...Thank you for a script which meets our needs for theatre-in-the-park."**—Dr. Fannie E. Hicklin, Professor of Theatre, University of Wisconsin-Whitewater